D0279676

Praise for *Facedown*

'*Facedown* is a unique and brilliant book. Matt's teaching and poetry informs the mind and warms the heart.'

Mike Pilavachi,
Director, Soul Survivor UK

'*Facedown* is a beautifully crafted and poetic book. But much more than that, it's a profound insight into the glory of God. While reading this book, often I would have to place it down and humble myself before the Lord. I was left challenged, convicted and inspired. This is a devotional book that I'll want to read again and again.'

Tim Hughes,
Author, *Here I Am to Worship*

'So often we focus on the joy we feel from the Father's love and forget to stand in awe of His majestic, almighty presence. In *Facedown*, Matt invites us to experience another side of worship, reminding each of us to worship in spirit and in truth in awe of our almighty God.'

Darlene Zschech,
Author, *Extravagant Worship* and *Kiss of Heaven*,
Songwriter and Worship Leader

Books by the same author include:

The Unquenchable Worshipper
The Heart of Worship Files

FACEDOWN

Matt Redman

survivor

Unless otherwise indicated, biblical quotations are from
the New International Version © 1973, 1978, 1984
by the International Bible Society.

ISBN 1 84291 188 0

Published by
KINGSWAY COMMUNICATIONS LTD
Lottbridge Drove, Eastbourne BN23 6NT, England.
Email: books@kingsway.co.uk

Designed and produced for the publishers by
Bookprint Creative Services, P.O. Box 827, BN21 3YJ, England.
Printed in Great Britain.

Dedicated to my amazing son, Noah Luca.
God heard our prayers and in His mercy restored
your breath. May you use that breath to live, speak,
and sing for the glory of God.

Thanks

Thanks to my beautiful wife, Beth – I love journeying with you – your passion and vision inspire me. And to Maisey Ella and Noah Luca – you are wonderful gifts from God.

I'm so grateful to all the teachers and encouragers God has blessed us to walk with and learn from – Don and Katherine Williams, Mike Pilavachi, Louie and Shelley Giglio, Bishop David and Mary Pytches, Terry and Wendy Virgo, Peter and Susan Brookes, Bishop Graham and Jackie Cray, Will and Caroline Kemp, Chris and Charlotte Cocksworth, Chris and Barbara Jack, and Ian and Jane Prior.

A massive thanks to Andrew Philip and Ellie Redman – for carrying the load with humility and passion. Thanks to Barbara, Lesley, Sarah and Dave for all your support – especially during the frantic times! Lots of appreciation also to those labouring hard to resource the church – Les Moir, Jon Pac, Richard Herkes and all at Survivor, Bill Greig III, Bill Denzel and all at Regal Books, Peter York for a spirit of generosity, and all at EMI(CMG).

Lastly, to my lead worshipper friends – for friendships that help strengthen and sharpen. To name a few, Tim Hughes, Martin Smith, Chris Tomlin, Charlie Hall, David Crowder, Todd Proctor, Eoghan Heaslip, Graham Kendrick, Andy Piercy, Stuart Townend, Martyn Layzell, Kate Simmonds, Nathan and Lou Fellingham, Paul Oakley, Nathan and Christie Nockles, Terl Bryant, Gary Richardson, Tom Lane, Brenton Brown, David Ruis, Darlene Zschech and all at Hillsong.

CONTENTS

FOREWORD

There's no place on earth like being facedown before the God of the universe, and no one on earth I know more capable of leading us there than my friend Matt Redman. From the first moment I came in contact with Matt's music I knew his heart had been profoundly affected by glimpses of a great and glorious God. Now that I've come to know him well, it's clear such glimpses are the reason he's been so effective in leading a generation to pursue a kind of worship that's marked at once by both reverence and intimacy with God.

Worship always begins with God. Apart from His willingness to share Himself with us we would never see His face, being forever stranded from His intimate embrace. God wants to be seen and known by you and me. That's why all through the pages of Matt's book you'll find the thread of God's revelation – that God-birthed, God-initiated unveiling of His majesty and terrifying holiness that drops us to our knees, awakening our hearts again to the miracle of grace that allows us to live and breathe in His presence.

Without true glimpses of God we will invariably try to shrink Him down to our own size, rather than allowing even the tiniest taste of His infinite glory to stretch our minds and souls upward as we try to fathom His. That's why worship without revelation is so lackluster, dull and void of the awesome wonder that belongs to God alone – the kind of nearsighted worship we can comfortably offer standing up or sitting down. But when our eyes are opened to drink in His matchless beauty we are intrinsically drawn facedown to the ground – that place of worship where we are both secure and somewhat afraid, in love and in awe, bowed low yet somehow lifted high.

If you think about it, to fall facedown is to actually move closer to God. It's mysterious how that happens, isn't it? The pure light of God's radiance could instantly and easily knock us flat on our backs, a massive blast of intense holiness that leaves us dead in its wake. But somehow in God's mercy the opposite actually happens as the brightness of His face draws us closer as we fall at His feet.

Facedown is one of those books you're not going to want to put down, but at some point I pray you will. And when you do, I trust you'll find yourself enthralled with the God of these pages – seeing Him more clearly than you ever have before as your face presses hard against the floor.

Louie Giglio

FACEDOWN

Chapter One

When we face up to the glory of God, we soon find ourselves facedown in worship. To worship facedown is the ultimate outward sign of inner reverence.

Every posture in worship says something of both the worshipper and the one being gloried in. The raising of hands tells of a soul stretched out high in praise and the worth of the one being exalted. Joyful dancing interprets a grateful heart and points in adoration to the source of that joy. When it comes to expressing our worship, what we do on the outside is a key reflection of what's taking place on the inside. Out of the overflow of the heart we speak and sing, we dance and we bow. God reveals, and we respond. God shines, and we reflect. In the very same way, facedown worship is the overflow of a heart humbled and amazed by the glory of God.

Facedown worship always begins as a posture of the heart. It's a person so desperate for the increase of Christ that they find themselves decreasing to the ground in an act of reverent submission. A soul so captivated by the Almighty that to bend low in true and total surrender seems the only appropriate response.

On several different occasions the Bible allows us a glimpse into an open heaven. Each time is a window of revelation, through which we discover more of what worship looks like before the heavenly throne. And there's a whole lot of facedown worship going on. In Revelation 1, John encounters the risen and exalted Jesus, whose eyes blaze like fire and whose face is shining like the sun in all its brilliance. Overwhelmed to the core, he shrinks to the ground in reverence and fear. A few chapters later the elders too are falling down in holy devotion. And as we journey further into this heavenly flow of praise, we find even more facedown worshippers:

> All the angels were standing round the throne and around the elders and the four living creatures. They fell down on their faces before the throne and worshipped God . . . (Revelation 7:11)

The book of Ezekiel gives us another glimpse into an open heaven, and we find more of the same. The prophet beholds the 'appearance of the likeness of the glory of the LORD'. There can be only one response: 'When I saw it, I fell face down . . .' (1:28). The reflex of his soul was reverence and submission. Facing up to the glory of God, he soon found himself facedown in awe and astonishment.

Daniel gives us another Old Testament glimpse of this heavenly scene. He sees a vision of the Lord Almighty, whose face shines like lightning, and whose eyes blaze like flaming torches. Undone by this divine encounter, here's another worshipper who cannot stay on his feet: 'I bowed with my face towards the ground and was speechless' (Daniel 10:15).

So many clues as to what our congregational gatherings should look like are found in these accounts of the heavenly throne. When it comes to worship, the throne always sets the tone. Each time we gather together, we don't just journey to a church building, we journey before the very throne of God. To lose sight of this is to lose sight of the majestic in worship. Every kingdom has a king, and every king has a throne. And the kingdom of God is no exception. He is the King above all kings, and He has the throne above all thrones. There is no higher seat of authority, power and splendour in the whole of the universe. The elders bow low there, the angels encircle it, and the whole host of heaven arrange themselves around it (1 Kings 22:19). One day, a countless multitude, from every nation, tribe, people and tongue, will gather there (Revelation 7:9). As Ron Owens tells us, 'When we come to worship, we come to a throne . . . [and] everything else arranges itself around that throne.'[1]

Journeying through the Bible, we find a whole host of facedown worshippers. Abram becomes one as the Lord God Almighty appears to him (Genesis 17:1–3). Moses and Aaron fall facedown too, as they encounter His glory (Numbers 20:6). King David also adopts the posture, in an act of humble repentance (1 Chronicles 21:16). And, over-whelmed by the radiance of the transfigured Jesus, Peter, James and John are also found among the ranks of the facedown (Matthew 17:6). Throughout Scripture, countless worshippers meet with God, and soon re-posture themselves before His splendour.

And it's not only the willing who find themselves facedown in an encounter with the living God. In the book of 1 Samuel, the Philistine nation captures the ark of the Lord (1 Samuel 5:1–5). Unaware of the power involved with this embodiment of God's presence, they carry it into their temple and place it beside the idol of Dagon. Early next morning, they find the idol facedown on the ground before the ark of the Lord. As my friend Louie Giglio comments, if you find your god bowed facedown on the floor before another God, then it's time to get a new one! Somehow, the Philistines don't quite get the message, and have the audacity to lift Dagon up, putting him neatly back in place. Big mistake. The next day they arrive at the temple, and there's Dagon, back on the ground, facedown before the ark of the Lord. Only this time his head and hands have been broken off too – and he's lying in pieces.

No power set against our Almighty God can stand in His presence. And those who dare to set themselves up against Him are setting themselves up for a fall. It is a facedown fall.

A few years ago, I saw a powerful example of facedown devotion at a gathering in Memphis, Tennessee. Hosted by the Passion movement of college students, this was a sacred assembly – a time set apart to worship, fast and seek the Lord. Thousands of students gathered on the field that day to consecrate themselves and pursue the glory of God in the nations of this world. Large events aren't automatically the most profound, but this one truly was. There were moments of heightened celebration as we rejoiced in the Saviour. There were times of 'selah', where we quieted our hearts and let the stillness remind us He is God. And there were moments of facedown worship.

Part way through the day, I saw a sight I shall never forget. It was pouring with rain, and the ground was getting pretty saturated. Yet all around me were students, face to the ground in the dirt, offering up their lives to God. They were not concerned about the downpour or the mud – or even the fact they'd already been in that field for many hours. Here were a people consumed with the glory of God, and everything they saw of Him propelled them to their knees in an extended act of lowly worship. The movement called Passion lived up to its name that day. It was passion accompanied by reverence; celebration accompanied by submission.

We see this fusion of joy and reverence many times throughout the Bible. The second Psalm counsels us to 'rejoice with trembling' – to delight in the welcoming mercies of His great love, yet all the while quaking in the depths of our hearts at the astonishing beauty of His holiness. In the same way, in Psalm 95 we begin by singing for joy to the Lord, yet before long find ourselves bowing down low in worship. As Charles Spurgeon comments on these verses, 'Joyful noise is to be accompanied with the lowliest reverence.'[2]

My favourite example of this mix of celebration and awe is found in the book of Leviticus. The glory of the Lord appeared and fire came out from

His presence. When the people of God saw this, they 'shouted for joy and fell face down' (9:24). It is an amazing picture. It is the wow and the woe of worship. A joyful shout lifted high to celebrate the goodness of God, followed by an Isaiah-like woe as they tremble at His greatness.

There's a whole lot of shouting for joy to be found in some of our worship gatherings, but how much face to the ground devotion do we see? The Scriptures show us that the most profound and wholesome worship contains an element of both.

The beautiful news is this: when God draws near in worship, we don't have to head for the door – God loves to meet with His people. Yet sometimes it can be a pretty wise move to head for the floor, for we must stay ever mindful of the glory of the One we are encountering.

Yes, when we truly face up to the glory of God, we'll find ourselves facedown in worship. And every heart will have to face up to it sooner or later. C. S. Lewis, talking of the second coming of Christ, puts it brilliantly:

Christians think that He is going to land in force. We do not know when, but we can guess why He is delaying. He wants to give us the chance of joining His side freely. God will invade . . . But what is the good of saying that you are on His side then? When you see the whole natural universe melting away like a dream and something else comes crashing in. Something so beautiful to some of us, and so terrible to others, that none of us will have any choice left . . . it will strike irresistible love or irresistible horror into every creature. It will be too late then to choose your side. There is no use saying you choose to lie down, when it has become impossible to stand up.[3]

One day we will all find ourselves facedown in the worship of Jesus. Every willing and unwilling knee will be bowed in humility; every artificial power and authority forced to the ground, just like the crumbled idol of Dagon. Rebellious tongues will not merely be silenced, but will be urgently confessing that Jesus Christ is Lord, to the glory of God the Father. It will be impossible to stand up on that day.

THE OTHERNESS OF GOD

Chapter Two

Worship thrives on wonder. We can admire, appreciate and perhaps even adore someone without a sense of wonder. But we cannot worship without wonder. For worship to be worship, it must contain something of the otherness of God.

I've come to love that word 'otherness'. It's such a great worship word. A sense that God is so pure, matchless and unique that no one else and nothing else even comes close. He is altogether glorious – unequalled in splendour and unrivalled in power. He is beyond the grasp of human reason – far above the reach of even the loftiest scientific mind. Inexhaustible, immeasurable and unfathomable. Eternal, immortal and invisible. The highest mountain peaks and the deepest canyon depths are just tiny echoes of His proclaimed greatness. And the blazing stars above, only the faintest emblems of the full measure of His glory.

Many music critics note that the skill of songwriter Bruce Springsteen lies in his ability to take the everyday and the ordinary and make it sound extraordinary. Sometimes in the church we find ourselves doing the total opposite – we take the extraordinary revelation of God and somehow manage to make Him sound completely ordinary! We fail to communicate the sense of God's otherness. As Tozer puts it, 'Left to ourselves we tend immediately to reduce God to manageable terms.'[1]

Time after time the book of Isaiah reminds us of the uniqueness of God: 'I will not give my glory to another' (42:8); 'I am the first and I am the last. Apart from me there is no God' (44:6); 'To whom will you compare me or count me equal?' (46:5); 'I am God, and there is no other. I am God, and there is none like me' (46:9). In light of scriptures like these, I'm becoming more and more wary of worship songs that seem to make God merely sound like our equal. Once or twice people have shown me worship songs and said, 'This is great. The lyrics are so down to earth that you wouldn't even know it's singing to God. It could be a normal pop song or a love song.' Now, I guess the point they're making is for cultural relevance, and that's a good point to make. But there is a higher value in worship than cultural relevance. It is the glory of God. God will not be diluted, dumbed down or patronised. He rebukes worshippers in Psalm 50: 'You thought I was altogether like you . . .' (v. 21).

But He is not like one of us. He is utterly incomparable – He is beyond the furthest horizon of our imaginations. He is off the scale of our comprehension. We have merely known the shallows of the mighty deep.

A while back I bought my daughter a couple of little goldfish. I've never really been one for keeping pets, but I figured that these tiny creatures were probably quieter and tamer than most. So there they sat, up on the mantelpiece, apparently forgetting everything once every one-and-a-half times around the bowl. The very next day I found myself watching a documentary about creatures of the deep sea. Right down in the depths of the ocean, the camera was capturing the most fascinating images of wild fish and other strange sea creatures. I sat glued to the screen – so many varieties and so much untamed beauty. And there in the background were Maisey's little tame goldfish, doing yet another lap of the bowl.

Sometimes, in the church, I worry that we've

settled for 'goldfish bowl' worship. We convey a tame and domesticated God, and find ourselves stuck in the endless pursuit of the ordinary. But the call is to venture out into the ocean, to encounter the extraordinary and to explore the mighty depths of God. And though our earthly gathered worship times may never fully sound the depths of His glory, beware of those that don't even attempt to.

Back to Psalm 50 and we discover that God doesn't even need our worship: 'If I were hungry I would not tell you, for the world is mine, and all that is in it' (Psalm 50:12).

Do we detect a harsh tone in the voice of God here? Yes, we most certainly do. This is the voice of the all-sufficient King of the universe. He does not need to be sustained, supported or sponsored. He is not in urgent need of our offerings, like a TV charity appeal, urgently appealing for as many contributions as possible. As Spurgeon puts it:

Do men fancy that the Lord needs banners and music, and incense, and fine linen? If He did, the stars would emblazon His standard, the winds and the waves become His orchestra, ten thousand times ten thousand flowers would breathe forth perfume . . .[2]

The apostle Paul echoes the same truth in his speech to the men of Athens: 'He is not served by human hands, as if he needed anything, because he himself gives all men life and breath and everything else' (Acts 17:25).

The plain truth is this: God has absolutely no need of our offerings. In fact, every single thing our open hands bring to Him – whether a good deed, a tithe or a simple act of compassion – came to us first from His hand. Even the songs of praise we sing to Him use the very breath which God first gave to us.

The book of Romans hammers the point home: 'Who has ever given to God, that God should repay him?' (Romans 11:35). One of the biggest mistakes a person can make in life is to think that God owes them something. It destroys faith, and insults the sovereignty of God. There are some incredibly painful struggles in this life, and hard questions we may never fully know the answer to. Yet even in these dark hours we must accept that God is God, and as such He never owes us an answer. As the hymn-writer William Cowper put it, 'God is His own interpreter'.[3] We cannot work Him out, or force Him to fit into our way of thinking. He is high above our human understanding – high enough to see things that we could never see.

But the picture of God's otherness is only really complete when we add to the mix the reality of His outrageous grace. It's true that God does not need our worship. But there is a crowning beauty which completes this truth – that God loves our worship. God delights in an honest and heartfelt offering of worship. Dwell on that mystery for a moment. Here is the all-sufficient Creator of the universe, who could get along just fine without our little contributions. And yet He rejoices and delights in every adoring response to Him. It is the joy of a doting Father over a cherished child. It is the pleasure of a mighty King over a faithful and treasured servant. Just as we cannot begin to imagine the heights and depths of His great glory, so too we cannot begin to fathom out the infinite measures of His fatherly love and grace.

And as the ultimate affirmation of this heart of welcome, God has even paid the way for us to draw near to Him in worship. We've seen that everything we could ever offer to God in worship was provided by Him in the first place. But even forgetting the gifts themselves, the very means of our access into His presence is all of His own provision too. It is a gifted response. We could never enter in by our own efforts. We come to the Father on the merit of what Jesus has done. In light of the cross, the resurrection and the ascension we come through Jesus, and in Jesus, and with Jesus. And we come too in the power of the Holy Spirit.

So not only does God receive with delight gifts which belonged to Him in the first place – He also pays the costliest of prices for their delivery. In human terms, this seems a little strange. How can that be a meaningful gift? Surely the giver must pay the full price? But we cannot always measure God by our human standards. This extravagant act of grace is yet another reminder of His incredible uniqueness. His ways and His thoughts are way higher than we could ever imagine.

The more we delve into the otherness of God, the more we grasp the truth that worship is quite simply all about Him. A phrase we may have sung many times, but do we realise just how true it is for every aspect of this life? The whole of our existence – our creation, our salvation and our sanctification – is first and foremost all about God. Another journey to the book of Isaiah and we get the message, loud and clear: '. . . everyone who is called by my name, whom I created for my glory' (43:7); '. . . the people I formed for myself that they may proclaim my praise' (43:21); 'I, even I, am he who blots out your transgressions for my own sake' (43:25); 'I have refined you . . . For my own sake, for my own sake, I do this' (48:10).

The Lord God Almighty, Maker of heaven and earth, stands set apart from all others. We are the created and He is the uncreated. Around Him revolves and unfolds the story of His great and eternal glory. And, yes, right through the very heart of this epic narrative runs a beautiful thread of grace – He is the steadfast God of love, and there is mercy to be found on every page. Time after time we find ourselves amazed by the blessings He lavishes on us. Yet let's not be fooled into thinking that this story is all about us. It never has been, and it never will be. God is very passionate about His own glory.

Some of us might find this a little hard to compute at first. Every day we see mere humans making claims to fame and boasts of their glory. And this can make it harder to get our heads around the fact that God must care about His own glory. But we must not confuse displays of earthly arrogance with God's declarations of His glory. It is not at all the same as boxer Muhammed Ali in his prime, ranting and raving around the ring screaming 'I am the greatest! I am the greatest!' and self-proclaiming his name and title. For sure, he had his time as a champion, but like all other mere men, he could not hold on to his crown. The boasts of men are motivated by pride and pure arrogance. They are empty, temporary and shallow. The claims of

God flow from glory and pure holiness. And they are powerful, eternal and true. For God to be God, He must care about His own glory. God must prize Himself above all else, for to prize anything or anyone else more highly than Himself would compromise His worth, and therefore imply that He is not God after all. As J. I. Packer puts it:

> If it is right for man to have the glory of God as his goal, can it be wrong for God to have the same goal? If man can have no higher purpose than God's glory, how can God? . . . The reason it cannot be right for man to live for himself, as if he were God, is because he is not God. However, it cannot be wrong for God to seek His own glory, simply because He is God.[4]

In the book of Isaiah the Lord declares, 'How can I let myself be defamed? I will not yield my glory to another' (48:11). He will never give up His title or yield His supremacy. He is untouchable, invincible and eternally glorious. In our celebrity-obsessed culture, fame rises up and then fades away – one minute someone has it, the next minute they're nowhere to be seen, and someone else enjoys or endures their 15 minutes' worth. God, on the other hand, will never allow Himself to be defamed, nor will he let His glory pass on to another. He is the undisputed, heavyweight King of all glory. In Psalm 66 the writer cries out: 'Sing the glory of his name; make his praise glorious!' (v. 2).

In recent times so much of the church has been inspired to make the praises of God more passionate, and also more intimate. And this is all vital ground for the singing church to recover. Yet there's also a call to make sure His praise is glorious. One of the biggest challenges facing a lead worshipper in these days is somehow to help the people of God find a voice to respond to His otherness. We need poetry, rhythms, visuals and melodies that will help us to sing the glory of His name: offerings which make it clear we are approaching the One who is high above all others.

One beautiful way of conveying this is to offer to God that which we do not spend on any other.

I love the lead up to Jesus' entry into Jerusalem, when He sends His disciples to a certain house to fetch a 'colt which has never been ridden'. It speaks of the otherness of the Son of God: the means by which He will be ushered into the city has been reserved for Him and Him alone. We must make sure that we find ways of doing the same in our congregational worship – finding ways of responding to God which we've reserved for Him only.

In the Old Testament, God gave the people instructions on how to make up a special anointing oil for use in the Tabernacle. He makes it clear that this oil is only to be used for worship – it must not be used for cooking or any other purpose: 'It is sacred, and you are to consider it sacred' (Exodus 30:30–33). We too must make room for the sacred in our congregational worship – responses which we use exclusively for God and no other. Take, for example, the act of bowing facedown. As we saw in the last chapter, this is a thoroughly biblical response in worship. And, in our Western culture at least, this is a physical gesture which we do not offer to any other – which makes it a fantastic response to the 'set apartness' of God; an act of reverence reserved for His praises only.

This principle must go far beyond our church gatherings and seep into the very fabric of our everyday lives; to treasure up words, thoughts and deeds we will only ever use in response to the Lord. In the past I've wondered if the fact that we have words in Scripture which are not now in common usage might be a big hindrance to cultural relevance. I'm starting to think that, used well, they might also be a great strength. Take the word 'holy', for example – a word that conveys the notion of one who is set apart. The very fact we only ever use it in the context of God and His church is a pretty appropriate thing. Now obviously there's a balance to be found – too many uncommon words and we start presenting a barrier to the uninitiated. But, accompanied by teaching on their meanings, these distinctive names and descriptions of God might actually be a powerful tool. Our culture is making up new words all the time. How fantastic if the worshipping church were to recapture a few old

ones as yet another way of conveying the uniqueness of God.

Out of reverence for Yahweh, the Jewish people
would not even inscribe the vowels when writing
down His holy name – a way in which, even in their
writings, they could convey something of the otherness of God. A while back I decided that every
time I type or write a word which refers to God
(Him, His, He, etc.), I will use a capital letter. It's
just one tiny way in which I can reflect something
of the otherness of God. By doing this, every time
I sit down to write a song – or any sentence to or
about God – I'm reminded of His holy otherness.
Reverence for God must find its way into even the
smallest details of our lives.

It's time for the singing church to once again
encounter the beautiful otherness of God. But we
cannot sing of that which we have not seen. In yet
more wise words from A. W. Tozer: 'What the
church needs today is a restoration of the vision of
the Most High God.'[5]

Spoken nearly half a century ago, this insight
seems just as relevant to us today.

MYSTERIES SO BRIGHT

Chapter Three

The God we worship is clothed in mystery. He reveals and He conceals. He invites and He hides. He confounds and He confides. The God who rests but never sleeps; who thunders and whispers, terrifies and befriends; whose anger lasts only a moment, but whose favour lasts a lifetime. All-consuming, yet kind. All-knowing, yet capable of forgetting the sins He forgives. The God who wounds and binds up, who injures and heals. The King whose footstool is the earth, yet who humbly washed the earth from the feet of those He discipled. Who reigns in righteousness, yet carried our shamefulness. Who walked in the Garden of Eden in the cool of the day, yet sweated drops of blood in the Garden of Gethsemane one agonising night.

The God of the smallest detail and the grandest design, who issued ornate designs for an extravagant temple, yet found pleasure in the humblest offering of a widow's two tiny coins there. The suffering servant who commands the universe. The sinless friend of sinners. The Saviour who hung in agony on beams of wood He Himself had called into being. Fearsome, yet welcoming. Unfathomable, yet knowable. The God of kings and beggars, presidents and paupers. Who fathers the fatherless and works through our weakness. Burning with holiness, yet refreshingly graceful.

He who is worshipped by the multitudes of heaven, yet rejoices over a single returning heart. Perfect in every way, yet able to help those who are being tempted. He who is faithful even to the faithless, for He cannot disown Himself.

This is the God we worship – the God of all mystery.

These days there's no mystery to life. Internet search engines try to convince us we can know anything and everything at the mere touch of a button. Reality television shows invite us to get up close and personal with an individual's life otherwise veiled. And at the other end of the spectrum many scientists strive to explain away God, and kick mystery out of the whole equation.

Sometimes I worry we're in danger of kicking mystery out of worship too. I've been a lead worshipper for a while now – half of my life in fact – and for the last ten years I've been trying to write congregational songs too. The more I journey on in these pursuits, the more I'm looking for ways to paint a bigger and more mysterious picture of God. So often I feel I'm doing the worship equivalent of taking holiday snaps on a disposable camera. The pictures are full of joy and intimacy (a good thing I think), but lacking in depth and mystery. I long to find fresh and meaningful ways to respond to the mysteries of our God.

Many lead worshippers I meet are on the very same quest. My friend David Crowder says, 'I want to build cathedrals. I want to use words and notes rather than stone and mortar.'[1] The challenge to those of us involved in leading others in worship is to write songs and build worship services which reflect majesty and mystery. I once heard the theologian N. T. Wright comment at a lecture given at Westminster Abbey that our English cathedrals are 'visual statements of the grandeur of God'. If you've ever entered one, you'll know exactly what he means. The grand architecture, the detailed craftsmanship and the sheer vastness of the building point to a God who cannot be fathomed or explained. As

Crowder goes on to say, 'Here they built to resize you upon entrance. They forced your gaze upwards. They surrounded you with beauty.'[2] Oh for more songs and services that do the same. Liturgies that resize us. Lyrics that force our gaze upwards. And inspired melodies that surround us with splendour, telling of the beauty of His holiness.

I once visited Notre Dame cathedral in Paris. As I entered the building they were blasting out a huge great anthem on a pipe organ, using some of the scariest chords I've ever heard in my life! The impact was amazing. I'm no expert on pipe organs in worship, but one thing I do know: when you get one of those things going full speed ahead, they resonate with an amazing sense of wonder and grandeur. And the music that day painted a picture of a God who is mightily mysterious, and mysteriously mighty. Whether it's organs or guitars, choirs or drums, the church today needs songs and sounds that echo the Almighty.

Each time we gather together as a worshipping community, we must find ways to reflect these aspects of the nature and character of God. The songs are one thing, but it goes way beyond the music. It's our whole approach. Are we preparing our hearts for a divine encounter? Too often I'm guilty of a rushed prayer with the worship band and a 'business as usual' mindset. But God does not delight in fast-food spirituality. This is a spiritual occasion, which must be marked by mystery and wonder. And you cannot rush into wonder.

In the Old Testament, as the people entered the Tabernacle to worship, they were given a very strong sense of what kind of God it was they were approaching. The whole design of this Tent of Meeting gave some very strong signals as to who they were worshipping and how they should worship. The Tabernacle spoke of a holy God, with an intense desire to dwell with His people. The white tented walls spoke of His purity. The ornate embroidered wall hangings spoke of the beauty of God. The very layout itself, with restricted access into the Holy of Holies (once a year for the High Priest only) spoke of God as a consuming fire, who must be worshipped acceptably with reverence and awe. The brazen altar conveyed the essential ingredient of sacrifice in worship, and the bronze lathe told of the need for the people to purify their hearts before approaching. Everything about the Tabernacle prepared the people's hearts for reverent worship.

Today we live under a new freedom. God is as holy as He ever was, yet through the perfect sacrifice of His only Son, we now enjoy the new covenant privilege of a close encounter with the Father. So to merely re-create the Tabernacle each Sunday would not be the most appropriate approach. Having said that, there is much we can glean from it for our congregational worship today. Just as the Tent of Meeting prepared people for the worship of God, do our meetings today help people get their hearts ready to bring a meaningful offering? Does our worship make it obvious what sort of God we're approaching, and how we should respond to Him? Do we convey the need to come with a pure heart, in light of God's holiness? Do our songs and services encourage people to draw near with reverence and awe? And are there ways we can communicate the beauty of God to those preparing to worship? Marva J. Dawn sums it up: 'The question is whether our worship services immerse us in God's splendour.'[3]

John Piper preaches that

> God meets us in high and holy ways. He meets us in lowly and meek ways. He meets us in thunderously glorious ways; he meets us in quiet, intimate ways. He meets us in complex ways and simple ways, furious ways and merciful ways.[4]

Notice how much of his observation revolves around opposites. So often paradox is the gateway to mystery and wonder in worship. If you take just one half of a mystery, it's no longer a mystery. As Jürgen Moltmann says, it's only in relation to the wrath of God that we know the mercy of God.[5] In other words, you cannot fully appreciate mercy until you recognise wrath. There are so many paradoxes found in the truths of Scripture, and each of these beautiful tensions is an essential ingredient for mysterious worship.

The greatest mystery of all is the cross. In fact, at Calvary we find many mysteries. The mystery of Jesus, fully God yet fully man. The mystery of mercy triumphing over judgement. At the cross we consider both the kindness and the sternness of God – or as Luther put it, 'Holiness and love kiss in the cross.' Isaac Watts, in his hymn 'When I survey', gets to grips with some of the paradoxes found at Calvary. The place where love and sorrow meet. The place where thorns compose so rich a crown. The place where we count our richest gain as loss. Even the opening line itself is full of mystery, 'the wondrous cross', for how can an instrument of execution be described as wonderful?

Another important mystery to embrace is the immanence and transcendence of God. In His immanence, God draws close to us and gets involved with our lives. In His transcendence, He is altogether otherly and self-sufficient. But for the mystery fully to ignite we need both of these elements held together in a beautiful tension. He is the God of the infinite and the intimate. We could watch Him from afar and for ever be amazed. Yet in his kindness God has drawn us near to Himself – and here the wonder is greater still. As theologians Olsen and Grenz explain it: 'God is immanent within human experience as the transcendent mystery that cannot be comprehended in spite of its absolute nearness.'[6]

In other words, when we truly draw near to God, our sense of His greatness and might will always be heightened, never diminished. Any sort of worship that esteems drawing near to God yet somehow portrays Him as merely a tame and cuddly friend perhaps isn't quite as near to Him as it would like to think. As Tozer puts it, 'No-one who knows Him intimately can ever be flippant in His presence.'[7] Look through Scripture, both Old and New Testament, and you'll find worshippers overwhelmed to the core in the intimate yet fiery presence of a holy God.

As we journey near in worship, our hearts of reverence for God will beat stronger and faster than ever. Up close and personal, yes. But also up close and unfathomable. As William Barclay points out, even in these incredible new covenant times where we may draw near to God, 'The New Testament is never in the slightest danger of sentimentalizing the idea of God.'[8]

The question is, are we?

THE WHOLE CHRIST

Chapter Four

I find it inspiring to read through the earthly accounts of Jesus in the gospels, and then flick straight to the heavenly description of His glory found in the last book of the Bible. We encounter Jesus as fully human yet fully divine. Many find it easy to picture the man Jesus, found in the gospel writings of Matthew, Mark, Luke and John. And it's crucial to feed on these amazing accounts of Jesus' 33 years' walking the earth. But if we're to grasp the bigger picture, it's essential also to feast on the revelation Scripture gives us of the eternal, glorified King Jesus.

In the book of Revelation He is revealed as the bright Morning Star, the First and the Last, the Beginning and the End. He is the triumphant Lion of Judah. He is the ruler of the kings of the earth, crowned with many crowns. With justice He judges and makes war. His eyes are like blazing fire, His feet like glowing bronze, and His mighty voice like the sound of rushing waters. Yet within the very same passages we encounter Him as the Lamb who was slain. Christian worship must contain both the cross and the crown.

In the seventeenth century, Richard Sibbes encouraged worshippers everywhere to 'take whole Christ' and not to 'divide Lord from Jesus, and so make a Christ of their own'.[1] When we encounter the whole Christ we find an incredible mix of power and patience, glory and grace. He speaks in words of both tenderness and toughness, rebuking the hard heart, yet welcoming the broken sinner. There is a certain kindness in His majesty. Christ is neither a hard taskmaster nor a soft touch. To the woman caught in adultery He spoke words of tender discipline: 'Neither do I condemn you . . . Go now and leave your life of sin' (John 8:11). He is easy to please, but hard to satisfy – the smallest offering of an honest heart will bring Him pleasure, yet He also has an insatiable desire to see us live out lives of utmost holiness.

One way to gain a greater glimpse of 'the whole Christ' is to reflect on some of the names and titles Jesus is given throughout the Scriptures. As Graham Kendrick comments on the many names of Christ revealed in Scripture: 'Each one is a key to who we are worshipping and why. Worship is a response and will grow or shrink in direct proportion to our view of Him.'[2]

He is the Light, the Life, the Way and the Truth. He is the Word made flesh – Emmanuel, God with us. He is the Hope of Glory, the Good Shepherd of our souls. When we start paying more attention to some of the names of Jesus, it opens the eyes of our heart to an even deeper realisation of His wonders.

As well as an abundance of names and titles in Scripture, we also find many different pictures of Jesus. So often we cling solely to images from the New Testament, but the challenge is to broaden our vocabulary and communicate Christ from the whole of Scripture. The Old Testament gives us so many symbols and foreshadows of Jesus which enrich and deepen our worship.[3] A Hosanna Integrity spoken word piece walks us through every book of the Bible and shows us how the Scriptures resonate throughout with different pictures of the Son of God. Here are some of them:

In Genesis Jesus is the Ram at Abraham's altar. In Exodus He's the Passover Lamb. In Leviticus He's the High Priest ... In Job He's our Redeemer that ever liveth. In Psalms He is my Shepherd and I shall not want ... In Isaiah He's the Suffering Servant ... And in Daniel He is the Fourth Man in the midst of a fiery furnace ... In Zechariah He is our Fountain. And in Malachi He is the Sun of Righteousness with healing in His wings ... In 1st Corinthians our Resurrection. In 2nd Corinthians our Sin Bearer ... In 1st and 2nd Thessalonians He is our Soon Coming King ... In Titus He is our Blessed Hope ... And in Revelation, lift up your eyes, Church, for your redemption draweth nigh, He is King of Kings and Lord of Lords.[4]

Each of these pictures gives us an even deeper understanding of the nature, character and ways of the God we worship.

As we seek to embrace the whole Christ in our worship, we do so in the context of worshipping God as Father, Son and Holy Spirit. At times this must be explicit in our song choices. But whether obvious through a certain lyric, or simply implied, an understanding of the Trinity should underpin everything we sing or say in our worship gatherings. In reality, 'understanding' is far too strong a word, for here on the earth we will never fully grasp the wonderful mystery of God in three persons, the Holy Trinity. Yet we must rise to the inspiring challenge of delving as deep as we can.

The more we immerse ourselves in this mystery, the more we realise there are many different dimensions to worshipping God as Father, Son and Holy Spirit. Chris Cocksworth calls it the 'Trinitarian geography of Christian worship'.[5] Yes, we praise Jesus the Son with everything within us, but we also join with Jesus in worship as He glorifies His Father. As the Holy Spirit reveals the lordship of Jesus to the depths of our hearts, He also takes us into the Son's relationship with the Father. Wow!

Worship is to Jesus, yes – absolutely. We glorify

the Son and magnify His name. But worship is also in Jesus and through Jesus and with Jesus. When Jesus walked this earth and willingly suffered the cross, His heart was to bring glory to the Father, and His mission was to bring us to Him. Now seated in the heavens at His Father's right hand, the heart and the activity of Jesus have not changed. He still glorifies the Father, and brings us with Him, and in Him, as He does so. We worship a glorious Father, a glorified Son, and the Holy Spirit of God, who, as one of the traditional ancient creeds reminds us, is also 'worshipped and glorified'.[6]

When our heavenly Father receives our worship, He receives it in the person of His Son, and in the power of His Holy Spirit. Our offerings are not complete in and of themselves. They only become perfect and acceptable acts of devotion on the basis of what Jesus has accomplished at the cross. As Harold Best puts it, 'While the believer offers, Christ perfects.'[7]

As we delve into these mysteries of Trinitarian worship, it is important that we allow them to remain just that – mysteries. The tendency can be either to sink into a pit of confusion as to how 'worshipping the Trinity' works. Or else to over-simplify things and attempt to sum up how it all fits together in a mere sentence. The bottom line is this: worship is a mystery. A glorious, heavenly mystery. When we come to worship the living God, we get involved with something far too deep for our minds to comprehend. As the writer to the Hebrews tells us,[8] we have come to God, the Judge of all, to Jesus the Mediator of a new covenant, and to the sprinkled blood that speaks a better word than any other claim we will ever hear upon this earth. We have come to the city of the living God, to thousands and thousands of angels in joyful assembly. The more the big picture comes into view, the more we realise just how small a piece of the whole canvas we really see. The worshipping life is an exciting pilgrimage into the depths of God.

WORSHIP WITH A PRICE

Chapter Five

When we catch a vision of the whole Christ, it commands a response from the very depths of our being. Worship is always in reply to revelation. As we begin to see the all-deserving worth of God, it produces an all-consuming response in us – every thought, word and deed submitted in reply to His lordship. It is worship with a price, a living sacrifice.

In Genesis chapter 22 God tells Abraham to journey to the mountain of Moriah, and there build an altar to worship Him. But this is no ordinary worship time. God instructs Abraham to take his son Isaac, for he is to be the offering. And though God never intends to let Abraham go through with this, the incident illuminates some important truths about worship. Ironically, one of the main insights comes from the boy Isaac himself. As they reach the appointed place and build an altar there, he says to his father, 'The fire and the wood are here, but where is the lamb for the burnt offering?' In other words, 'Everything seems as if it's in place, but where's the sacrifice?' That is always a key question when it comes to real and meaningful worship: 'Therefore, I urge you . . . in view of God's mercy, to offer your bodies as living sacrifices, holy and pleasing to God – this is your spiritual act of worship' (Romans 12:1).

We would do well in our worship to ask the same question the boy Isaac asked – where is the sacrifice? Sometimes in our worship meetings the 'fire' and the 'wood' are there – in other words, outwardly everything seems to be in place – and we think we're set for 'great worship'. A skilled music team perhaps, or above average songs and an enthralling preacher. But something is missing. Where is the sacrifice? Now, I'm not for one moment suggesting that we try to have a miserable time in our church services – quite the opposite. In one sense, worship should be the most enjoyable thing on earth. In fact, as John Piper reminds us, God is most glorified in us when we are most satisfied in Him. But what I am suggesting is that there must be times in our worship services when we cease to say, 'Please give me more,' and we start to say, 'It's time I gave you more.' Moments where we journey from 'Here I am, meet me' – as wonderful a prayer as that can be – and move on to complete the integrity of our worship by crying, 'Here I am, send me.' Sometimes in our worship gatherings, the only thing left to do is go.

Mission is the ultimate example of worship with a price. Mission is love on its feet, running for the glory of God, no matter what the cost. It flows from a passion for God's name and a desire for His glory to be known in the whole of the earth. As Piper reminds us, 'Missions begins and ends in worship.'[1] Worship is the fuel for mission's flame – praise propels us onto the mission field, whether near or far. And worship is also the heart of mission's aim, for effective mission produces more worshippers of Christ.

I recently had the privilege of meeting Heather Mercer, a missionary aid-worker who was captured by the Taliban and imprisoned for many days. Stirred up by a passion for God and a compassion for His world, Heather had travelled out to Afghanistan on a worship-fuelled mercy mission. Not long after beginning the aid work, she and her friend Dayna Curry were arrested and imprisoned by the oppressive Taliban regime. Their story is an incredible account of honesty and endurance, and tells how trust-filled hearts of worship for God fuelled them through this intense ordeal.

On meeting Heather, I was humbled to learn that during her time in captivity she'd sung some of our worship songs. To be honest, it was more than humbling – it actually made me feel pretty awkward. I couldn't help but compare her adventurous, persevering missionary experience with my relatively safe lifestyle as a musical lead worshipper. It's one thing to write a little worship song, but it's another thing completely to sing out a faithful offering while held captive by the Taliban. Most of the time, there's no price to penning a song. But to live and sing out songs of trust and devotion while in captivity is a far more costly matter. Please don't misunderstand. As far as I can discern, part of what I'm called to do in life is to write worship songs, and I'm not attempting to belittle that. Or anyone else who does that. But the point is this: the call on all of our lives is to journey beyond melodies and harmonies, beyond lyrics and poetry.

The fact is, people like me sometimes end up getting a bit too much attention. It's something that happens when you start doing things up the front at church. And every time I come across the likes of Heather Mercer, I receive a Holy Spirit wake-up call. A reminder that worship goes far, far deeper than the strumming of an acoustic guitar. In the same sentiment as King David, I will not sacrifice that which cost me nothing (2 Samuel 24:24).

The call of Christ is to a radical life of love and service – a life which leads to many costly acts of devotion. Intimacy with guts. Passion with perseverance. Not everyone will be a Heather Mercer. Some are called specifically to the foreign mission field. Others are called to show up at the office on time, and faithfully represent Christ and His kingdom in the workplace environment. William Barclay gives a fascinating insight into this, in the lives of the brothers James and John. He tells of the occasion when Jesus asked these two disciples if they could drink the cup which He Himself must drink, and they replied that they could. Jesus tells them a time is coming when indeed they will (Matthew 20:22–23; Mark 10:37–39). As Barclay writes:

So, then, both of the brothers drank the cup of Christ. Let us see what that cup was. John went to Ephesus; he lived for almost a hundred years; and died in peace full of years and honour. James's life was short, and came to an end swiftly and suddenly through martyrdom by the sword – and yet both drank the cup of Christ. There is a Roman coin which has as its inscription the picture of an ox facing an altar and a plough, with the words: 'Ready for either.' The ox must be ready for the dramatic sacrifice of the altar or the long routine of the plough. The Christian who dies in one heroic moment, and the Christian who lives a long life of fidelity to Christ both drink the cup of Christ. The Christian . . . must be ready for either.[2]

Another expression of worship with a price is to trust God even through the dark nights of the soul. Trust is a beautiful and costly act of worship – an honouring response to the sovereignty of God and His fatherly heart. An old hymn expresses this truth powerfully:

Can a child presume to choose where or
  how to live,
But can a Father's love refuse all the best
  to give?[3]

In other words, we cannot choose our path in life, but we can choose to walk down it with a worshipful trust in the sovereignty and Father heart of God.

A couple of years ago my wife Beth and I wrote a song called 'Blessed be Your name'. Touching on the book of Job, the song aims to convey the call to worship God in both the bright and dark seasons of the soul:

You give and take away, You give and take
  away,

My heart will choose to say, 'Lord, blessed
   be Your name.'[4]

When writing this song, I began to realise it
was a song with a cost. These are words you cannot
sing lightly, for the price is too high if you do not
believe them. Whether we sing looking back over
our past, or in view of all that may unfold in the
future, there is a price tag attached – an intense
fusion of trust, abandonment and, ultimately, sacrifice. Since writing this song we've had letters
from people struggling with some of the harshest
life circumstances I've ever come across. And
whether they face grief, loneliness or the aftermath
of abuse, all these worshippers have one thing in
common. They are choosing to turn their faces to
Jesus and say, 'Though there's pain in the offering,
blessed be Your name.'[5]

I have an American friend whose sister recently
passed away after a long battle with cancer. This
friend of mine is one of the best lead worshippers
I know. Having seen him lead worship just weeks
after his sister so painfully passed away, I now

think I know why. It wasn't anything he sang or said – though his songs are some of the most profound around, and musically he does something very fresh. But that day up on the stage, he set an inspiring example for the believers to follow. In the midst of heartache and the agonising 'why' questions that sometimes stir in us, he stood up and proclaimed the worth of God for all to see. He did not deny the pain, but stood in the midst of it looking upwards to the unchanging glory and love of God. There was pain in the offering. He then began to lead us in the old hymn 'On Christ the solid rock I stand':

> When darkness seems to hide His face,
> I rest on His unchanging grace.
> When all around my soul gives way,
> My anchor holds within the veil.[6]

The next day I sat with him over coffee, and he told me, 'That's my song at the moment.' My friend Charlie, in the midst of great pain and the shifting sands of life, was choosing to stand on the solid rock of Christ and celebrate Him. A powerful picture of worship with a price.

One of the best examples I've come across of a man who sang his worship passionately, yet backed up his songs with a life of devotion, was the founder of the Salvation Army, William Booth. With a heart set on mission and mercy, Booth lived out his love for God through a life of serving the poor – a life so fruitful that we still feel its repercussions all over the world today. So what was the secret to Booth's success? Was he a focused visionary, following the seven key steps to building a long-lasting ministry? Was he an insightful planner, carefully working out a global strategy master plan which would establish the Salvation Army around the world for decades to come? No, I don't think so. Booth himself knew the key to his fruitfulness in ministry. It was worship with a price:

> I will tell you the secret. God has had all there was of me. There have been men with greater brains than I, men with greater opportunities. But from the day I got the

poor of London on my heart, and caught a vision of all Jesus Christ could do with them, on that day I made up my mind that God would have all of William Booth there was. And if there is anything of power in the Salvation Army today, it is because God has had all the adoration of my heart, all the power of my will, and all the influence of my life.[7]

At the age of 83, just before he died, he gave his last public address at the Royal Albert Hall:

While women weep as they do, I'll fight, while little children go hungry as they do now, I'll fight, while men go to prison, in and out, I'll fight, while there yet remains one dark soul without the light of God, I'll fight; I'll fight to the very end.[8]

The most meaningful and powerful worship always comes at a price – the whole of our lives placed on His altar.

THE SONG OF CREATION

Chapter Six

The Bible shows us time and time again what a special role music has to play in helping us communicate devotion to God. Throughout the Old Testament we're shown many pictures of the gathered people of God using music to convey their worship. We're even given a whole songbook – 150 psalms of passionate prayer and praise. The New Testament is a little more sparing with these accounts of congregational music, and we're only provided with a few hints to keep us on the right scent – talk of psalms, hymns and spiritual songs, and making music in our hearts to the Lord (Ephesians 5:19; Colossians 3:16).

But then we arrive at the last book of the Bible, and here we find the most inspiring pictures of all – congregational music filling the throne room of God with pure and creative worship. The poet and hymn-writer Christina Rosetti once commented that in Revelation chapters four and five 'Heaven is revealed to earth as the homeland of music'.[1]

In these chapters we're also reminded that musical praise is not just found on the lips of mankind. Before the heavenly throne we hear every creature in heaven and on earth, and under the earth, and on the sea, and all that is in them, singing (Revelation 5:13). In fact, the more we search through the Bible, the more we encounter the song of creation. On many different occasions the Scriptures describe the musicality of creation as it responds to the Creator:

> The seas have lifted up their voice . . .
>   (Psalm 93:3)

> Let the sea resound, and all that is in it; let the fields be jubilant . . . Then all the trees of the forest will sing for joy . . . (Psalm 96:11)

> Let the rivers clap their hands, let the mountains sing together for joy . . . (Psalm 98:8)

> The mountains and hills will burst into song before you, and all the trees of the field will clap their hands. (Isaiah 55:12)

A while back I visited the Natural History Museum. The exhibits themselves were interesting enough, but the main education experience for me happened in the museum shop at the end of my visit. I came across some CD recordings of different types of 'nature music' – the sounds and tones of various creatures, such as wolves and whales, mixed in with some background piano music. It was an interesting concept, and I found it surprising to hear just how musical a sound some of these creatures made. One thing bugged me though: these CDs were being released on a New Age label. Something is wrong there, for these sounds do not belong to the New Age movement. They are the sounds of creation as it responds to the one true God of Ages. As Francis of Assisi expressed it 800 years ago in song: 'Let all things their Creator bless, and worship Him in humbleness.'[2]

Creation is alive with musicality, and every sound, note and strain is a response to the divine, pointing to the Author of all life – God Himself. A few years back I watched *The Rhythm of Life*, a BBC documentary series presented by former Beatles producer Sir George Martin. In one episode he interviews Bernie Krause, a musician who spends his life out in the wild, recording the sounds of nature. Krause is amazed by the seemingly 'orchestrated' musicality of the natural world, and plays Martin a fascinating recording – exploding cells in a tree, popping perfectly in time, with an incredibly sophisticated and pretty rhythm. As Krause explains:

> After a long period of time when there's no water ... and then suddenly there's a downpour, the dry cells which make up the trunk begin to expand very quickly. And when enough of them explode, it puts out a very high pitch tone, which causes that kind of rhythm.[3]

In fact they take this beautiful rhythm recording and have one of the world's top percussion players play along with it. Everyone in the room is quite clearly stunned by just how intricate and perfectly in time these exploding tree cells are.

We find another example of creation's musicality in the synchronised rhythms of South American ovenbirds. When male and female Hornero birds burst into song, the male voices around six notes a second, and then gradually speeds up the tempo. Yet instead of keeping up with her partner, the female ovenbird complements his beat with her own interesting rhythm. Singing perfectly in time, despite the speed of the song, they create a beautifully intricate song.[4]

The music of creation is all around us. From the tiniest atom, to the greatest spiral galaxy, every moment since the dawn of creation, nature has been ringing aloud with the glorious praises of God.

Psalm 19:1–4 tells us:

The heavens declare the glory of God; the skies proclaim the work of his hands. Day after day they pour forth speech; night after night they display knowledge. There is no speech or language where their voice is not heard. Their voice goes out into all the earth, their words to the end of the world.

Then, in the New Testament, Romans 1:20 takes on the same theme and tells us:

> . . . since the creation of the world God's invisible qualities – his eternal power and divine nature – have been clearly seen, being understood from what has been made, so that men are without excuse.

As Bob Dylan testified:

> I can see the Master's hand
> In every leaf that trembles,
> In every grain of sand.[5]

In a loud and clear voice, creation proclaims the works, and ultimately the worth, of an incredible designer. The more we delve into the beauty of nature's design, the more we hear it reverberating with the splendour of the Creator. Scientists these days coin phrases such as 'the fine tuning of the universe',[6] 'the dazzling order of the universe',[7] and 'nature's irresistible mathematic patterns'.[8] Many times what impacts these scientists most is that things so structurally complex could also be so inherently beautiful. To the atheist mind, these are happy coincidences. But to the burning heart of a worshipper, they are yet more fuel for the fire.

You don't need to look far to be amazed by the intricate designs of creation. Our very own bodies bear witness to the wonders of our Creator. Each of us contains around a trillion cells, of more than a hundred types, knitted together in a very complex manner.[9] Our hearts pump the equivalent of 1,800 gallons of blood a day.[10] Our brains process roughly 100 million pieces of data each second, yet use far less electricity than a light bulb to do so. We can hear over 300,000 different tones, and see approximately 8 million colour differences. As for our muscles, if all 600 pulled together in one direction, we would be able to lift around 25 tons of weight.[11]

And then we start to look beyond ourselves,

into the rest of the created order, and everywhere we look we find amazing displays of His splendour. From the vast expanse of a star-filled sky, to the intricate design of a butterfly wing, creation acts as a signpost, pointing us in praise towards our Maker. Psalm 148, one of the great creation psalms, gives us a good example of this. The poetic truth of this psalm is powerful in and of itself, yet to mix it up with some modern-day scientific findings is a fascinating exercise.

In the third verse the psalmist declares, 'Praise him, sun and moon.' Looking at this sentence through a scientific lens gives us some fascinating insight, for every second the sun burns up 4 million tonnes of its own mass, releasing energy equivalent to 100 billion hydrogen bombs exploding. And as a clue to just how massive it is, though losing this 4 million tonnes of mass each second, scientists still estimate the sun will last another 5 or 6 billion years.[12] The sun brings us light and heat, yes. But more than anything the psalmist sees it as a proclaimer of the great and unending worth of God. Praise Him, sun!

Later in the same verse, the writer of Psalm 148 cries out, 'Praise him, all you shining stars,' and looking through our scientific lens once again puts this verse into a fascinating context. For our sun, although enormous, in the wider scheme of things is actually just a very average-sized star – one of around 200 billion in our galaxy, the Milky Way.

Think for a moment about the scope of that. Only 6,000 stars can be seen from the earth by the naked eye, and of these only 2,000 from any one point. In a well-lit city we'll probably see no more than a hundred. But even on this level, anyone who's ever gazed into the night sky will have recognised the grandeur of it all. Yet we see only the tiniest glimpse of the true reality out there. There are hundreds of billions of stars in our galaxy alone, and astronomers now think there to be at least 140 billion other galaxies, many of them bigger than ours.[13] Scientists estimate that in the visible universe alone there are ten times more stars than there are grains of sand on all the world's beaches and deserts.[14] Take a deep breath . . . and worship. We are smaller than we ever thought. And far more importantly, God is greater than we had ever imagined.

On one level, we may say that a star shines because it is converting hydrogen into helium in its core, in a process called nuclear fusion. Scientifically, that's correct and, let's face it, pretty amazing. But the psalmist here has an even more astounding insight for us – first and foremost the stars are shining in praise of the One who spoke them into being: 'Praise him, all you shining stars'!

And it's not just the sheer scope of creation which fills us with praise for the Creator. The wonders of God's handiwork are to be found in the tiniest details of all He has made. One powerful example of this beauty is in the intricate design of a snow crystal. Anyone who's seen snowflakes under a microscope cannot help but be amazed by how beautifully complex they are. I recently came across the story of Wilson A. Bentley, the 'snowflake man' born in the late nineteenth century, who coined the phrase, 'No two snowflakes are the same'. Bentley devoted nearly 50 years of his life to the study and photography of these 'fragile jewels'.

Fascinated both scientifically and artistically by snow crystals, he marvelled at what he called the 'wondrous beauty of the minute' in nature. As he observed from the 5,000 photographs of snow crystals he collected: 'Under the microscope I found that snowflakes were miracles of beauty . . . Every crystal was a masterpiece of design, and no one design was ever repeated.'[15] Yet another reminder of the wonders of the Creator.

For those ready to listen, the song of creation is all around us, declaring the glory of God. Alister McGrath writes, 'It is part of the purpose of the creator that we should hear the music of the cosmos and, through loving its harmonies, come to love their composer.'[16] With every blast of splendour, and every ray of beauty, creation is not exalting itself. Every snowflake that falls to the ground, and every star that shines above, tells of the glory of God. It is the song of creation. The more we hear this song, the more it points us once again towards the 'otherness' of God. He is both the author and the receiver of this magnificent orchestration of praise. The sun, the moon, the stars, the hills, the fields, the trees, the seas, the angels, the elders, the living creatures – everything! All joining in one song – the eternal anthem of the Almighty.

THE SOUND OF
SHEER SILENCE

Chapter Seven

There's a time for every kind of sound when we gather together to worship God through music. A time for majestic anthems, and a time to quietly whisper His praise. A time for dancing in abandoned celebration, and a time for stately chords that speak of holy splendour. Yet there is also a time when the most appropriate response is simply to be still – and in that stillness know that He is God.

Tozer wrote that, in some instances, absolute silence might well become our greatest act of worship.[1] The book of Revelation tells of a holy silence in the worship of heaven (Revelation 8:1), and so too in our earthly devotions we must mark out moments for stillness and reflection in the presence of God.

A few years ago we were recording an album of new worship songs in the south of England. One night we invited a group of 15 drummers and per-cussionists into the studio for an evening of worship. We were hoping to journey somewhere special in worship, more than anything seeking to have 'church' together in the studio environment.

We hit 'record', forgot about all the technical stuff, and started playing a simple idea I'd had a few moments earlier, now called 'The prayers of the saints'. What followed was 20 minutes of free-flowing, spontaneous worship. And then something beautiful happened. We drew to a close, and stood there in silence, finding ourselves deep within the presence of God. There were over 20 people in that studio, yet not one person spoke a word. Every heart instinctively knew that this was not a time for playing or saying anything, or a moment to launch into another song. This was a time for sacred silence – we were encountering the living God.

Usually there'd be some technical questions flying around at this point – 'Was that a good "take"? Shall we go for one more?' – and all the usual studio jargon. But tonight everyone knew such talk wasn't appropriate. In fact, not one person in that room even mentioned the recording side of things that night. There we stood in stillness, instinctively knowing how offensive to the Lord a question like that would be in a moment like this. The presence of God puts life into perspective.

The prophet Habakkuk declares, 'The LORD is in his holy temple; let all the earth be silent before him' (Habakkuk 2:20). As Andrew Murray says, 'The very thought of God in His majesty and holiness should silence us.'[2] We still our hearts and silence our tongues in wonder and reverence before a holy God. And often these moments of stillness take us even deeper into Him, creating essential space for us to hear the voice of God. As we quieten our souls in response to His glory, they are opened further to perceive even more of His holy radiance. Silence in worship contains elements of revelation and response. In stillness we both honour and behold God.

When it comes to congregational worship, there are perhaps two types of silence. The first kind is the most sacred of moments, where we sense heaven touching earth, and the Holy Spirit ushers us into an encounter simply too weighty for words. The other kind is an uncomfortable 'pregnant pause', which causes us to squirm – and long for a song (any song!) to fill the embarrassing void. The discerning lead worshipper quickly learns to distinguish between the two, and respond appropriately. One reason we seem afraid to embrace moments of prolonged stillness in our congregational worship is that we have not effectively responded to these two types of silence in the past.

Many churches have given up on looking for moments of sacred stillness because they have been burned by too many unappointed and uncomfortable pauses. Our culture in general has little time for quietness, and faced with moments of stillness, many of us rush in to fill the space, not knowing how to handle it. As congregations we need to learn to follow the promptings of the Holy Spirit. As the ultimate worship leader, He will at times lead us into the presence of God through the gift of sacred silence.

We also need to carve out moments of hushed beholding in our daily lives as individuals. In Psalm 131:2 the writer talks of quieting his heart before God, or as *The Message* phrases it, 'I have cultivated a quiet heart.' I love that term. Cultivation speaks of working to create an environment of stillness in our hearts and lives. Moments where we block out all distractions, and simply reflect on the beautiful revelation of God. I once heard Bill Hybels, pastor of Willow Creek Church in Chicago, teaching on a question he often asks himself: 'Is the ambient noise level of my life low enough for me to hear the whispers of the Lord?'[3]

That's a great question for any follower of Christ. There are so many different types of noise in our lives which drown out the essential soul-strengthening ingredient of stillness. Josef Pieper, in his book *Only the Lover Sings*, puts it like this:

Man's ability to see is in decline. Searching for the reasons we could point to several things: modern man's restlessness and stress . . . or his total enslavement by practical goals and purposes. Yet one reason must not be overlooked either: the average person of our time loses the ability to see because there is too much to see.[4]

There is so much to see and hear in this busy and media-flooded world of satellite television, home cinema and the internet. We need seasons of the soul where we somehow find space away from the noises of everyday life, and still our hearts to perceive the intimate whispers of God.

I recently found one such moment. We were having the roof of our house repaired, and had some scaffolding running up the outside wall of our house. One evening, as the sun was setting, I took the opportunity to climb up onto the roof and grab a few moments of stillness and reflection. No phone. No TV. Not even any people. Just me and God. Up on that roof I realised a principle that's true for both the natural and the spiritual life: the higher you go, the more you see. Sounds obvious, but it's an important principle for us to grasp. Up there, far above the street, I saw beautiful views of the surrounding area that I'd never seen before. We must make it our aim to climb higher, spiritually speaking. To find moments and places where we may rise above the noise of twenty-first-century life and give space for reflection. As a general rule, too much time at the television or the Playstation will not help us climb higher. If we want to scale greater heights and see further in God, we must find moments where we ascend above every distraction and find an unobstructed view of Him.

Speaking honestly, I find this one of the greatest challenges in life. And more often than that, the main barrier to cultivating a quiet heart is just a matter of personal discipline. Too often in moments of leisure I find myself instinctively reaching for the remote control and flicking through the most meaningless of TV programmes. And if my wife Beth challenges me on my use of time, I'll simply say I'm 'relaxing' – that all-important Western world excuse for apathy. But recently, the writings of the fourth-century Desert Fathers have been teaching me a lot about the personal discipline needed to carve out these moments of stillness. Their ruthless approach to the spiritual walk with God is both inspiring and scary. Inspiring, because they have much to teach us about spiritual discipline. But also scary, because sometimes they seem to go a little overboard in their zealous pursuit of these disciplines!

Take Father Abba Agathon, for example. They say that for three years he carried a pebble around in his mouth until he learned to be silent.[5] Now that's a pretty extreme approach to cultivating a quiet heart. As well as being a slightly anti-social practice, there are obviously some hygiene issues too! But, the way I see it, if some guy can keep a stone in his mouth for a thousand days, the very least I can do is turn off the music channel for a few minutes. As one of the Egyptian Fathers teaches: 'You need a spiritual pilgrimage. Begin by closing your mouth.'[6]

Having studied the lives and practices of these Desert Fathers, Anselm Gruen gives us the following insight: 'In silence the inner disturbances can quiet down, the dust cloud can settle, to let the heart clear up. It is like cloudy wine, which becomes clear after lying quietly in storage.'[7] Silence is a great environment to see and hear God.

One man who encountered God in the stillness was the prophet Elijah. Burned out in every way, in 1 Kings 19 we find him in a dark night of the soul, and in desperate need of a touch from God. Here's a man who has scaled the heights of powerful ministry, seeing miracle after miracle and the breakthrough of God in the most challenging of circumstances. But in this passage we find him in a far from victorious state of mind. He is, quite frankly, in depression. And then God speaks. But not through the shock of an earthquake, the force of a powerful wind or the theatrics of a mighty fire. God speaks to Elijah in a still small voice (vv. 12–13), or as the New Revised Standard translation so powerfully phrases it, in 'the sound of sheer silence'. What a beautiful and mysterious thing – to hear the whisperings of God in the sound of sheer silence.

The God of glory, who thunders over the mighty waters, reveals Himself intimately and quietly to the depths of our hearts. When alone, and when gathered as a worship community, we must learn to listen out for Him – in the sound of sheer silence.

AWESTRUCK

Chapter Eight

When our eyes are opened to the big picture, and we catch a greater glimpse of God, we are awestruck. The otherness of God, His wonderful mysteries, the view of the whole Christ, the song of creation and the sound of sheer silence all lead us in one direction – awe. Facedown worshippers throughout Scripture all have one thing in common: an awesome view of God.

That word 'awesome' is one of the most misused words in our current culture. These days, anything vaguely exciting is described as awesome. Everything from the special effects of the latest blockbuster to the taste of a fast-food hamburger is apparently awesome – or, quite literally, worthy of awe. We'll hear fanatic fans tell their celebrity heroes, 'I'm in awe of you,' but this cannot be the case, for if they truly were in awe, they would be flat on their faces. The Bible tells us that awe is something reserved for God, and God alone: 'Dominion and awe belong to God' (Job 25:2).

What a thought. We know that honour, praise, glory and power belong to God. Yet here we learn that awe too is reserved for Him alone. We may stand inspired or impressed by the characteristics and achievements of another human being, but – in the correct sense of the word – we must never stand in awe of that person. Awe is reserved for God alone. It is the look of wonder and amazement that flows from one who has glimpsed God in His splendour.

The Bible tells us, 'The highest angelic powers stand in awe of God. He is far more awesome than those who surround His throne' (Psalm 89:6–7, New Living Translation). In other words, the radiance of the angels, as bright and beautiful as that may be, is far outshone by the glory of God. Yet angels are by no means unimpressive beings. Many times in Scripture they strike fear and astonishment in the hearts of those they appear to. We would quite simply be overwhelmed in their presence. In Revelation 18:1 one lone angel lights up the earth with his allocated splendour. Another time in the Old Testament we hear of a single angel putting to death 185,000 men in the enemy camp (Isaiah 37:36). Pretty formidable stuff.

And yet angels – and there are millions of them – fall on their faces before the heavenly throne, and worship the Lamb of God for His glory, honour and power (Revelation 7:11–12). These glorious beings, so impacting that they inspire fear and trembling in the hearts of those who see them, bow down in their multitudes at the sight of the One who is altogether more glorious. They are but a created reflection – just the tiniest hint of the true radiance of their Maker.[1]

If we look at the early church, one of the keys to their power is that they were awestruck. The book of Acts tells us, 'Everyone was filled with awe' (2:43). These first Christians were inspired by the resurrection and empowered by the Holy Spirit. Yet we're shown another factor here in their effectiveness to shine as the people of God in this world: they walked in awe of God. These followers of Jesus had seen the big picture – a God glorious enough to spend the whole of their lives on, and powerful enough to uphold them as they did so. They had seen enough of His glory and love to risk their lives for the cause.

A look at the deaths of the disciples (as detailed in *Fox's Book of Martyrs*) gives us a powerful demonstration of this. James, son of Zebedee, was beheaded for his faith. Andrew was crucified, as were Philip, Bartholomew, Jude and Simon Zelotes. Matthias was stoned to death in Jerusalem. Simon Peter was crucified upside down. And James the Less had his brains beaten out with a club at the age of 94. Many of the other disciples and early followers of Jesus were also tortured and martyred for their faith.

Their courageous choice to persevere was a response to the revelation of the worth of God. They had encountered Jesus – the nearness of His friendship and the power of His resurrection. They had seen the glory of His ascension, and now lived and moved in the sustaining power of the Holy Spirit. They had seen enough to endure.

Look through the history of the church and you'll find many extraordinary worshippers who lived with this grand view of God. Awestruck at the sight of the Almighty, divine encounters lead us to lives of passionate and powerful kingdom ministry. Take, for example, John Wesley. His journal entry on 1st January 1739 reads:

> Mr. Hall, Hinching, Ingham, Whitefield, Hutching, and my brother Charles were present at our love feast in Fetter Lane with about 60 of our brethren. About three in the morning as we were continuing instant in prayer the power of God came mightily upon us, insomuch that many cried out for exulting joy and many fell to the ground. As soon as we were recovered a little from the awe and amazement at the presence of His majesty, we broke out with one voice, 'We praise Thee, O God, we acknowledge Thee to be Lord.'[2]

These awed and amazed worshippers went on to change the spiritual climate of a nation. In the early eighteenth century, Britain was in a terrible condition – drunk on gin and morally corrupt. The church was filled with deism, and Christianity in the nation had, according to Bishop Berkeley, corroded 'to a degree that was never known in any Christian country'.[3]

In this spiritual climate, Wesley travelled continuously throughout Great Britain, preaching the gospel in prisons, workhouses, chapels and fields, and covering close to a quarter of a million miles by horseback as he did so.[4] Along with George Whitefield and others, he was greatly used to bring about a revival affecting every class of society. As Archbishop Davidson wrote in 1928, 'Wesley practically changed the outlook and even the character of the English nation.'[5]

The life of Jonathan Edwards gives us another great example of an awestruck worshipper:

As I rode out into the woods for my health, in 1737, having alighted from my horse in a retired place, as my manner commonly has been, to walk for divine contemplation and prayer, I had a view that was for me extraordinary, of the glory of the Son of God, as Mediator between God and man, and His wonderful, great, full, pure and sweet grace and love, and meek and gentle condescension. This grace that appeared so calm and sweet, appeared also great above the heavens. The person of Christ appeared ineffably excellent with an excellency great enough to swallow up all thoughts and conceptions . . . I felt an ardency of soul to be . . . full of Christ alone; to love Him with a holy and pure love; to trust in Him; to live upon Him; to serve Him and to be perfectly sanctified and made pure, with a divine and heavenly purity.[6]

A vision of Christ shaped Jonathan Edwards' life, and his life and ministry went on to shape the church, even society itself. It was Edwards' powerful preaching that God used as a catalyst for the Great Awakening – a series of powerful revivals that swept through New England, USA, in the mid-eighteenth century. And many of Jonathan Edwards' inspired teachings still impact us to this day.

We too need an encounter. As a writer of

worship songs, I have a hunger to write deep songs of passionate reverence to God. Yet I'm aware I cannot sing before I have seen. All worship is a response to a revelation – it's only as we breathe in more of the wonders of God that we can breathe out a fuller response to Him. Whether a banker, a musician, a pastor or a schoolteacher, the key to a life of passionate and powerful worship comes from seeing God. The more we encounter Him, the more impacting our lives will be. As A. W. Tozer said,

> If the Holy Spirit should come again upon us as in earlier times, visiting church congregations with the sweet but fiery breath of Pentecost, we would be greater Christians and holier souls. Beyond that, we would also be greater poets and greater artists and greater lovers of God and His universe.[7]

We live as worshippers of the otherly in a culture of the ordinary. Society today attempts to explain everything. But when it comes to worship, not everything can be explained. In worship, explanation gives way to mystery. And mystery leads us to reverence and awe. We are to worship with understanding, but never complete understanding. Who can fathom the depths of the God we worship? Who can describe His unapproachable light? Who can predict His wonderful ways? Who can measure the depths of His love? As we gaze upon the Lord in worship, we are drawn into this mystery. We run out of ways to describe the indescribable. Who can sound the depths of glory? Every single song falls short. No poetry says it well enough. No melody expresses it beautifully enough. Our lives themselves become the song. And we become awestruck worshippers, living every note of our existence in response to His glory.

God is stirring up His church again with a holy urgency to delve deeper into the soul-gripping wonders of who He is. We have heard many new sounds, and we have heard many new songs. And, thank God for them. But it's time now for a new sense in our songs and sounds. And in the whole of our lives. A sense of wonder. A reverent intimacy, and an intimate reverence. Where friendship underlines fear, and fear underpins friendship. Where rejoicers tremble, and tremblers rejoice. Holy poetry, biblical love songs and anthems of His goodness and greatness. More than anything, the call is for lives lived out in holy obedience and facedown submission – our greatest possible response to the glory of God.

And then one day we will join with the great multitude of facedown worshippers. On that day, as we sing with the countless choir of the redeemed, we'll find ourselves facedown before the King of all glory.

AFTERWORD

Matt has been brave enough to allow me the last word! This is a powerful and vital book. In a few short chapters he has demolished a stereotype of charismatic worship and outlined its potential.

As different traditions and practices of Christian worship develop, they take on distinctive characteristics. So traditional cathedral worship is thought to convey the grandeur of God, charismatic choruses to convey intimacy with God, songs from Scotland's Iona community the earthiness of serving Christ in the world, and so on. It would seem that the answer would be to mix and match from different styles and traditions if we are to convey the breadth and depth of God in

Christ and worship Him as He deserves. The trouble is that this ends up with acts of worship which lack coherence, where everyone endures elements they neither like nor feel they can express from the heart. A better strategy is to expand the scope and vocabulary of each tradition so it more adequately carries the breadth and depth required of all Christian worship.

However much renewal worship may be stereotyped, the power of stereotypes is that they are usually based on some truth. So Matt has also written an important challenge to the weaker aspects of the renewed worship tradition, and, for that matter, of most other worship traditions as well. This is a book for all worshippers, not just for lead worshippers.

In particular Matt's book reminds me of a number of crucial things.

That Christian worship involves personal intimacy with God, but that intimacy is with the holy God who is not like us, even though we are made in His image. In the language of theology, we have intimate relationship with the transcendent God.

That worship is 'in the Holy Spirit'. The wonder being that, through the cross, the holy God dwells in me, and I am enabled to respond to Him in love. That awe and intimacy are inseparable.

That worship is not just about cultural accessibility, although God in Christ has entered our world. It is about the transformation of our way of seeing into God's way of seeing, our perspective to God's perspective.

That worship is not escapist – it does not evade pain and suffering, and the test of its authenticity is the life of service which results.

That worship is not just about experiences, although encounter with God lies at its heart. It is also about character. As Richard Foster has said in his book *Celebration of Discipline*: 'To stand before the Holy One of eternity is to change.'

Finally our worship can never, in this life and perhaps in the next, plumb the depths of Christ. Worship cannot exhaust Christ, nor dare it try to make Him manageable – when you see Him as He is, you fall facedown.

As you reach the end of this book, I advise you to read it again – slowly.

Bishop Graham Cray

NOTES

Chapter 1
1. Ron Owens, *Return to Worship* (Broadman & Holman, 1999), p. 53.
2. Spurgeon, *The Treasury of David*, Vol. 2 (Thomas Nelson, 2002), p. 166.
3. C. S. Lewis, *Mere Christianity* (Fount, 1983).

Chapter 2
1. A. W. Tozer, *The Knowledge of the Holy*, p. 20.
2. Spurgeon, *The Treasury of David*, Vol. 1 (Thomas Nelson, 2002), p. 387.
3. William Cowper, 'God moves in a mysterious way'.
4. J. I. Packer, *Hot Tub Religion* (Tyndale, 1987).

5. A. W. Tozer, sermon on 'Prayer', Chicago 1956, quoted in *Worship and Entertainment* (Christian Publications, 1998), p. 54.

Chapter 3

1. Davidcrowderband.com
2. *Ibid.*
3. Marva J. Dawn, *A Royal Waste of Time* (Eerdmans, 1999).
4. Copyright ©1997 John Piper. Extract of talk notes from Bethlehem Baptist Church, 28th December 1997, posted on www.desiringgod. org
5. Jürgen Moltmann, *The Crucified God* (SCM, 1974).
6. Olsen and Grenz, *20th Century Theology* (IVP, 1997).
7. A. W. Tozer, *That Incredible Christian* (Christian Publications, 1986) p. 129.
8. William Barclay, The Letter to the Hebrews, *The Daily Study Bible* (St Andrew Press), p. 187.

Chapter 4

1. Richard Sibbes, 'The Bruised Reed and the Smoking Flax', 1635, from *Works of Richard Sibbes, 1862–4* (James Nichol).
2. Graham Kendrick, www.heartofworship.com
3. I am grateful to Vineyard pastor Rich Nathan for sharing this challenge at a songwriting and theology retreat.
4. Copyright Hosanna/Integrity Music 1993.
5. A lecture given by Chris Cocksworth at London Bible College, September 2003.
6. I am indebted to Revd Chris Cocksworth, Bishop Graham Cray, Revd Chris Jack, Don Williams and Robin Parry for various teachings and conversations on Trinitarian worship which have helped me in this section.
7. Harold M. Best, *Music through the Eyes of Faith*, pp. 155–6.
8. Hebrews chapter 12.

Chapter 5

1. John Piper, *Let the Nations be Glad* (IVP, 2003).

2. William Barclay, *The Master's Men* (Northumberland Press Ltd, 1959), p. 101.
3. Laurence Tuttiet, 'Father, let me dedicate' (hymn).
4. 'Blessed be Your Name', Matt and Beth Redman ©2002 Thankyou Music.
5. *Ibid.*
6. 'On Christ the solid rock I stand' (hymn by Edward Mote).
7. www.times1190.freeserve.co.uk/general.htm
8. www.born-again-christian.info/vision.htm

Chapter 6
1. Source not known.
2. 'All creatures of our God and King', Francis of Assisi, 1182–1226.
3. *The Rhythm of Life*, BBC television series, episode 1.
4. *The Guardian*, 8 January 2004.
5. 'Every Grain of Sand' by Bob Dylan, © 1981 Special Rider Music. All rights reserved. Int. copyright secured. Reprinted by permission.
6. Bob Berman, *Discover* magazine, 2003.

7. Steven Strogatz, 'Sync'.

8. Ian Stewart, *The New Mathematics of the Living World* (Wiley, 1998).

9. Ian Stewart, *Life's Other Secret* (Penguin, 1999), p. 15.

10. Bill Bryson, *A Short History of Nearly Everything* (Broadway Books, 2003).

11. The above four facts (brain/ears/eyes/muscles) come from Thomas Subay, *The Evidential Power of Beauty: Science and Theology Meet* (Ignatius Press, 1999), pp. 231–2.

12. *Ibid.*

13. Bill Bryson, *op cit.*

14. Andrew Craig, BBC Online, 07/03.

15. Duncan C. Blanchard, *The Snowflake Man* (The McDonald and Woodward Publishing Co).

16. Alister McGrath, *The Re-enchantment of Nature* (Hodder & Stoughton, 2003), p. 13.

Chapter 7

1. A. W. Tozer, quoted in Dick Eastman, *Heights of Delight* (Regal, 2002).

2. *Waiting on God, Meditations by Andrew Murray* (Ambassador, 1997), pp. 88–9.

3. Bill Hybels, sermon at Willow Creek Conference, 2001.

4. Josef Pieper, *Only the Lover Sings* (Ignatius Press, 1990).

5. *Desert Wisdom – Sayings from the Desert Fathers*, introduced by Henri J. M. Nouwen (Maryknoll & Orbis Books, 1982), p. 5.

6. *The Book of Mystical Chapters; Meditations on the soul's ascent from the Desert Fathers and other early Christian contemplatives*, translated and introduced by John Anthony McGuckin (Shambhala Publications Inc., 2002), p. 47.

7. Anselm Gruen, *Heaven Begins within You – Wisdom from the Desert Fathers*, translated by Peter Heinegg (The Crossroad Publishing Company, 1999), p. 58.

Chapter 8

1. I am indebted to Vineyard pastor Steve Nicholson for many of the thoughts in this paragraph.

2. *The Works of Wesley*, Third Edition, Vols 1 & 2 (Baker, 1998). Reprint of 1872 edition in London, Vol. 1, p. 170.

3. www.gospelcom.net – Glimpses Issue no. 38: Evangelical revival in Britain.

4. *Ibid.*

5. *Songs and Sermons: John Wesley and Charles Wesley* (Fount Classics), p. vii of intro.

6. D. Martyn Lloyd-Jones, *Joy Unspeakable* (Kingsway, 1984), pp. 79–80.

7. Source not known.

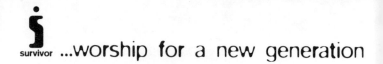
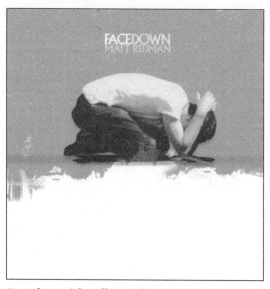